THE
REST
RACE

DEV MENON

GRACEW☐RKS

THE REST RACE

BY DEV MENON

The Rest Race
Copyright © 2019 Dev Menon

All rights reserved. No part of this publication may be reproduced, stored in a retrieval system, or transmitted, in any form or by any means, electronic, mechanical, photocopying, recording or otherwise, without the prior written permission of the author, except in the case of brief quotations embodied in critical articles and reviews.

Published by Graceworks Private Limited
22 Sin Ming Lane
#04-76 Midview City
Singapore 573969
Tel: 67523403
Email: enquiries@graceworks.com.sg
Website: www.graceworks.com.sg

Scripture quotations are from The Holy Bible, English Standard Version® (ESV ®), copyright © 2001 by Crossway, a publishing ministry of Good News Publishers. Used by permission. All rights reserved.

Scripture quotations marked "NIV" are taken from the Holy Bible, New International Version®. NIV®. Copyright © 1973, 1978, 1984, 2011 by International Bible Society. Used by permission of Zondervan. All rights reserved.

Scripture quotations marked "YLT" are taken from Young's Literal Translation by Robert Young, 1862, 1887, 1898.

ISBN: 978-981-14-0625-6

A CIP record for this book is available from the National Library Board, Singapore.

2 3 4 5 6 7 8 9 10 . 25 24 23 22 21 20

CONTENTS

- Foreword vii
- A Question 1
- It Starts with a Garden 5
- Unrest 11
- The Rat Race 17
- A Divine Interruption 23
- Show me the Manna 25
- Sabbath^{x7} 41
- A Crucial Interruption 45
- Unrest, Redux 47
- Re-Orientation 51
- Rest Fuel 53
- Selah 61
- Back to the Question 65

 | # FOREWORD

> I'm prepared to contend that the primary location for spiritual formation is in the workplace.

Thus, wrote Eugene Peterson.[1] Having been working for 15 years (seven years full-time in the Singapore Armed Forces, and eight years straddling the worlds of the marketplace and the church community as a bi-vocationalist), I fully agree with Pastor Eugene.
The workplace is the battlefield and graveyard of many a soul out of rhythm.

So, I gladly recommend this book as essential reading. It certainly reads like a book written by my dear friend, Pastor Dev. Out of his pastoral experiences, books spring forth. I figure he has seen, in his pastoral ministry, enough cases of folks who have deeply struggled with seeking purpose in their work. I see also that much has come out of his reflection on his own experience (pastoral work is hard work).

---

[1] In his acclaimed book, *Christ Plays in Ten Thousand Places: A conversation in spiritual theology* (Grand Rapids, MI: Eerdmans, 2005).

To think properly about work, Pastor Dev would baptise us into Scripture. He seeks to dislodge us from the world of EVIL-work that we've been cursed into, and then invites us into the blessing of the life-giving rhythms of Sabbath rest. All this without sounding pedantic.

Baby steps, but necessary ones...because we are prone to compartmentalising our life, which simply means that we automatically surrender to the fear and greed (i.e. SIN) that reign in the workplace. But we are in the business of integrating everything: making sense of life through the wisdom that God has already given to us and demonstrated in the flesh in Christ, and taking every thought captive to obey Christ (2 Corinthians 10:5).

After this, go ahead and read more on what it means to be image-bearers of a God who works and who is still working; and on what it means to exercise our powers for redemptive justice and righteousness, in other words, to do GOOD-work.

But first, learn to trust and obey.

Ng Zhi-Wen
Program Executive, Singapore Centre for Global Missions

 # A Question

Are we made to WORK or to REST?

Or how about I change the question to:

Do you WORK to REST or REST to WORK?

I think all of us are quite familiar with the question: "Do you live to eat or eat to live?" It's the same kind of question. It's not just a cute saying. The answer reveals something very deep—it shows us our true philosophy, what defines us. If we eat to live, then survival is our instinct. If we live to eat, then enjoyment is one of our #lifegoals.

What about the original question—do we WORK to REST or REST to WORK? How would you answer?

After living in both Asia and Europe, it's quite striking to see the different attitudes to work. Some people live to work, others work to eat, while others don't seem to want to eat or work.

Generally speaking (and yes, I know this is stereotyping), in the West, I saw people living as if 'work is a *means* to life'. They are trying to work hard enough—doing something they really don't like to do—with the goal of retirement, or to do something truly meaningful.

> Many of the postdocs I worked with when I was a scientist were just working hard enough so that they could buy a car, a house and have enough to do something exotic like head out to the 'Far-East' to become a diving instructor for the rest of their lives—to sit in the sun and drink cocktails. I used to think they were stark raving mad, especially because I could not imagine why anyone would want to sit in the sun on a voluntary basis.

In Asia, I saw mainly the opposite: 'work *is* life'. It is the defining identity of most, both male and female. Let these stories illustrate:

> A pastor once shared with a group that in his old corporate firm, the boss printed out 2,000 business cards one week before he retired. Now there was no way he would use that many cards, plus of course those cards would be completely invalid once he left the firm; they all said 'CEO' on them. So why did he print them?

> A group of friends once went out to help the

elderly-poor on the streets. They met an old lady who was folding cardboard boxes to sell them for a few cents per kilogram. It was backbreaking work for an 80+ year old! My friends offered to give her some money and to buy her a meal but she flatly refused. She said that she had very well-off children, and had a nice house to live in herself with a domestic helper to boot! So why was she there?

The relative of a middle-aged man who had been in a disabling accident asked him to move in with him so that he could take care of his needs. He had more than enough financially, and again had a domestic helper to manage all necessary tasks. The man moved in—since he had little choice—but then he refused to eat. When asked why, he said, "I can't work, I'm useless, I don't deserve any food."

Work was all-consuming. No work = No life.

So which way is right?

Should WORK define us and be the 'be-all and end-all' of our existence—something core to our identity? Is REST just the thing that we do in order to be able to do more WORK?

Or is WORK something temporal in order to earn our retirement? Is REST the objective?

Or is it something different altogether?

It Starts with a Garden

In the beginning, God created the heavens and the earth.

It is written that He worked six days and on the seventh day He ceased from His work of creating, and used the next day to rest,[1] setting up a pattern of WORK and REST for humanity to follow (as we will see later on).

But let's take a closer look:

Why did God create Adam & Eve only on the sixth day? Why not create them first, before anything else was made?

Well one reason is practicality I guess; they needed a ground to stand on (Day 3), air to breathe (Day 2), light to keep them warm (Day 1 and Day 4), so on and so forth.

---

[1] Genesis 2:1–3

But I think the reason that makes the most sense is because God saved the best for last. He wanted everything in creation to be ready for the climax—His precious children, Adam and Eve. God only created human beings when everything was completed; as soon as they were done, so was He!

The first activity that Adam and Eve experienced was God's blessing[2] (presumably on Day 6) and then God's resting on Day 7—the Sabbath Day. When Jesus (the One that walked in the garden) met them, it was described as a pleasant afternoon stroll in the garden;[3] He was enjoying the fruit of His work by resting with His new children. Adam and Eve were made, and the first thing they were made to do was to enjoy all of the finished creation-work, with the God who laboured over the last six days.

He was the one who worked really hard so that they could enjoy all His labour, with Him.

That's pretty much the standard thing with parents, right? We work really hard, so that we can get things ready for the children, who then enter into *our* life to enjoy *our* labour. *We work, they rest.* They don't have to do anything to earn their place. They start their lives much more in a position of REST—resting in their parents' WORK. But what about Adam? What WORK is Adam meant to do?

Let's slow that all down and zoom in on Genesis 2. Initially, human-work was not even possible because there was

---

[2] Genesis 1:28a

[3] Genesis 3:8

no rain.[4] The ground was watered through a mist which covered the whole earth.[5] I guess everything on earth grew naturally with no human effort—just divine irrigation.

Adam was then handcrafted by Jesus Christ, and kissed into existence, as his future Bridegroom breathed His life into his nostrils.[6]

Adam then must have witnessed God creating paradise (Eden) for him. Everything being made by the hand of God, handcrafted, and tailor made. A beautiful land filled with gold and precious stones flowing from the river that came from the mountain of God.[7] Then every tree, good for food and good for the eyes! Beauty and functionality coming together, all emanating from God's work and generosity.

Adam is then placed into the garden and given the gift of God's work to enjoy, on the day of enjoyment—the Sabbath Day.

Here comes the big question though. What was Adam made to do in this paradise garden?

> *The L*ORD *God took the man and put him in the garden of Eden to work it and keep it.*[8]

---

[4] Genesis 2:5

[5] Genesis 2:6

[6] See John's gospel.

[7] Where else did it come from if there was no rain?

[8] Genesis 2:15

Ah...so Adam's core function or identity is to do a kind of gardening work then?

But wait a minute. Didn't God do all the gardening already? What work exactly does Adam need to do? Horticultural maintenance? The garden is already great; it is called paradise, it produces fantastic fruit, plus— there is no rain! This doesn't seem to add up. Why does Adam need to work this park at all?

Well, let's look at another translation of that verse:

> And Jehovah God taketh the man, and <u>causeth him to rest</u> in the garden of Eden, to serve it, and to keep it. (YLT)

This version tries to translate the verb more literally: Adam was not so much 'placed' in the garden, but rather 'rested' in the garden. The same word is used in Genesis 19:16, where Lot is taken out of the chaos of Sodom and Gomorrah and placed safely outside its boundaries. The word 'placed' is a different word used from 'placed' in Genesis 2:8, and most dictionaries indicate it refers to being settled down in a nice new place (implying the last place was rather messy), i.e., to be quieted down.

The imagery to me is again one of a new child being shown into his new playroom, a place of safety and comfort where he can enjoy himself thoroughly without worry.

If Adam was 'rested' in the paradise garden, which has everything ready for his flourishing, what work does he have to do?

Well, the verse continues to state he has to '*work and keep it*', or '*to serve it and to keep it*'.

A little more language here. The verb 'to serve and to keep' is like a catch phrase in the Old Testament. For example, if I say 'to serve and protect', you would automatically think 'police' (if you watch American TV shows). 'To serve and to keep' was often in reference to priestly service.[9] When the two verbs are seen together (take Deuteronomy 13:4 and Joshua 22:5 for example) they refer to '*serving God and keeping His commandments*'.

Some theologians also suggest that this pair of words (serve and keep) cannot strictly be in reference to the garden because the 'genders' for the verb and the nouns do not agree (which needs to happen in a language like Hebrew).

I don't think Adam is asked to work the garden or steward the fruit trees per se, but rather, His 'work' is to serve God and obey Him! Which is why the next verse is:

> *And the* LORD *God commanded the man, saying, "You may surely eat of every tree of the garden, but of the tree of the knowledge of good and evil you shall not eat, for in the day that you eat of it you shall surely die."*[10]

---

[9] See Numbers 4.
[10] Genesis 2:16—17

We serve God and keep His Words. Adam sets up the role of God's people more as priests[11] than gardeners! We are to steward His Word and His Way, and of course earth-maintenance (creation care) comes into that framework,[12] but in that order.

Taking that together, we can see that Adam (and later, Eve) was placed in this beautiful paradise, not to work the ground (that comes later), but to enjoy the fruits of God's work for him. Just keep remembering that imagery of that little child placed into a beautiful parental home with every good thing given, and now asked to follow his Father's instruction.

God worked, Adam rested.

God created, Adam blessed.

God loved, Adam beloved.

All Adam's life came from God and would always continue to come from God. Adam starts in REST. I guess the thing Adam and Eve needed to do to keep the fruit and fellowship coming, was to trust God and learn His ways.

---

[11] For further reading see: G. K. Beale, *The Temple and the Church's Mission* (Downers Grove, MI: IVP Academic, 2004).

[12] For example, Deuteronomy 20:26.

 # Unrest

Obviously, that never happened.

Despite Adam having seen God plant every tree (note that Eve would have to rely on Adam's testimony)—each one beautiful to look at, each one full of sweet fruit; tasting rivers of clean water, surrounded by gold and jewels; seeing God bring all the animals to him and giving him dominion over them; exclaiming joyfully when a life partner was made from him and for him; experiencing a God that just kept giving and giving, blessing after blessing, providing for each and every need beyond all that he could ask or think of and imagine. Even then, it was not enough.

Surely Adam was supposed to infer from his creation experience the things that Jesus would teach us explicitly later: God is generous and lavish. God provides all we need. God is where we find our rest, our safety and our comfort. God is the source of everything good.

Surely the right response, was to 'lean back' and REST in the goodness of God. To joyfully sing this refrain:

> *Surely goodness and mercy shall follow me all my days of my life...*[1]

Trust Him, enjoy Him, have life through and with Him!

REST had nothing to do with sleep,[2] but much more with trusting, enjoying, living and experiencing God.

And yet,
>...Adam couldn't rest
>...Adam couldn't trust.
>...Adam fell.

As soon as Adam and Eve were satiated with all these good things,

> *...you forgot the God who gave you birth.*[3]

They began to forget that they were needy creatures who needed life from the Father. They began to think that they were quite independent beings, self-sufficient, in control of their own lives and destinies. Once they were happy, fat little children, they thought, "We are okay by

---

[1] Psalms 23:6

[2] Sleep in the Scriptures seems more to be associated with death than rest.

[3] Deuteronomy 32:18

ourselves. We don't need anyone else. Why not we be our own gods?" They thought they could orchestrate their own lives.

The snake pours doubt into the naïve ears of the children, and they begin to shift their eyes elsewhere. The result is written in stone; the words of the Fall are plain to read in Genesis 3.

They cut themselves off from God—His way, His truth, His life—and ventured out on their own. The prodigal son parable in the gospels gives a picture of this event. Abundant life is rejected and off we go.

It's like my kids when they hit the 'terrible two' stage. Despite giving them affection, a safe home, beautiful (and environmentally friendly) toys, the first word they often articulate clearly is "no", which often graduates to, "I don't want!" "Eat your vegetables son, they are good for you." "I don't want! I want lollipop!" The lunch plate goes flying off the table.

Just like that Luke 15 story, the son who has everything he wants and asks for does not seem to have enough; nothing makes him happy. There's a voice in his ears that turns everything good into deception and malice. The Father is a slave driver, a tyrant. The son's got to get out there and find independence.

God obliges. He allows his errant children to leave—out of the house. God's children are permitted to go and WORK to create their own life, a life that has been cut off, independent, isolated (or so they think) from the Father.

In the Genesis scenario, a flaming sword bars their return. They cannot return to Edenic rest-living any more.

Yet God still loves them, and so now the good discipline comes in...

> ...*cursed* is the ground because of you; in pain you shall eat of it all the days of your life; thorns and thistles it shall bring forth for you; and you shall eat the plants of the field. By the sweat of your face you shall eat bread, till you return to the ground, for out of it you were taken; for you are dust, and to dust you shall return... therefore the LORD God sent him out from the garden of Eden to work the ground from which he was taken.[4]

Adam is permitted to live out his own life, yes, but God will not let that way of life prosper. Adam (humanity) is not cursed, but the ground he will need to work to get life, is!

He would have to till the ground for food to survive, but the ground would fight him—it would hurt him. He would have to toil, sweat and labour. It would give him some sustenance, but only temporarily.

Ultimately, the dust will want its dust back.

You can try to build your Babel towers, but the Lord will confuse your work.

---

[4] Genesis 3:17–19, 23.

The Lord's curse is a universal "NO" to Adam's independent life; in everything he does, he will NOT live long and prosper. Toil, Sweat, Labour—this is our first *experience* of WORK (since there was none happening in Eden).

Even then, it is all futile. Work as hard as you want, climb as high as you can go…and you get nothing in return. You will still die. Everything you have accomplished will return to the ground you came from.

Toil, Sweat, Labour, Die.

No matter how much we try, no matter how much effort we put in, no matter how successful we become — everything we do is useless, everything beautiful is marred, and every good deed is contaminated. Imagine a wall that has cracks in it. And now the rain keeps getting in, and fungus and mould are growing, mildew sets in. You can keep putting new cement, you can keep painting it white again and again, but that doesn't get rid of the mildew. The rot within is growing and growing and growing—and there's nothing you can do about it. Best-case scenario: tear the building down and throw it away.

Jesus loves to use the analogy of a tree, poisoned to its core. What can you do to make a rotten tree bear good fruit? Nothing, absolutely nothing. Every branch, every stem, every leaf, every flower, every fruit—the toxins are in every vein. You can prune it to slow it down, but really, the only feasible option is to cut it down and throw it away. The more it grows, the worse it gets. This is our sorry state, and this is the reality of the curse. Our God-ordained destination is death, and then a second death—the cosmic rubbish bin, hell itself.

WORK post-Fall is motivated by a desire to be our own gods and gets a divine "NO!" to ensure its futility. It is EVIL-WORK.

 The Rat Race

WORK = The activity I need to do to get life.

No work...
　　　...no money
　　　　　...no food
　　　　　　　...no life.

Although Adam and Eve themselves quickly learn their lesson (they offer the blood sacrifice), most of us follow the way of Cain—and don't.

We become used to this idea of living outside of God's presence and providence. We like the idea of being our own masters, attempting to earn our own life through the work of our hands. I guess it's the only life we know!

As the generations press on, we believe that the more we work, the better it will get. Futility can be overcome by greater self-effort: If I just put in more effort, more time, more energy, do enough, strive enough, fight enough, increase intelligence, increase wealth, increase power—then I will have more life!

This is the EVIL-WORK logic. It is hard-wired into our thinking, that our own hands can bring us life. When we begin to factor in that we are not alone and there are other annoying humans to deal with, then what we call the 'rat-race mentality', sets in.

Values like competition, elitism and exclusiveness arise. With limited resources from a cursed ground, we have to fight off the competition. This results in a proliferation of violence—as we see the world descend into by Genesis 6 (we are still just as violent these days, especially with the virtual realm). On a national scale, this looks like social inequality, oppression, xenophobia, abuse and injustice of all kinds.

Dog-eat-dog, kill or be killed, you must be number one or...who are you? These are the vermin voices that plague our minds.

These don't just play out on macro-international levels, they happen even in spheres as small as the school playground. They are the defining interactions of the human community in every age and every culture. This is the rat race.

If we are lucky enough to succeed in this mindset, it leads to pride and arrogance. A sort of foolishness to think that we can go on perpetuating this way of life forever without consequences.[1] We forget about our impending death as we claim to be the masters of the universe.

If we are unfortunate enough to fail, the hostile earth gets the better of us, then life is plagued with anxiety and stress, despair and disillusionment. These can cement into depression, self-loathing, self-harm and even suicide. Surely it would have been better if I had not been born!

If we refer back to our Eastern stereotype, work becomes all-consuming and all-defining. Once we cannot compete, we lose all identity and worth and we become essentially useless, deserving only death. The effect of this on the less-abled is tremendous! Despair is inevitable in these cultures because surely the time will come when you cannot work. We secretly hope to die before retirement age comes a-knocking!

In the West, the only difference is to work hard enough so that I can enjoy non-work retirement long enough. I guess it does give meaning and value to human beings beyond their capacity for industriousness. Yet the irony is by the time we get our golden handshake, we are usually too old, too sick and too disillusioned, so there's nothing left to enjoy—and we can't wait for death to come fast enough.

For those that seem to be super-wealthy-elite, like those crazy rich Asians we hear about, often their celebrity status seems to only exacerbate the space between them

---

[1] See the parable in Luke 12.

and the next person—there is the constant refrain of deep loneliness—triggering drug abuse, depression and suicide.

The rat race is horrible.

We all know it, we all feel it. This way of EVIL-WORK, fuelled by our independence, exacerbated by the CURSE. One way or another, we have repeated moments of feeling like a stinky pig, eating waste products and longing for death.

No wonder Solomon called this meaningless, vain, a chasing after the wind:

> *Again I saw something meaningless under the sun: There was a man all alone; he had neither son nor brother. There was no end to his toil, yet his eyes were not content with his wealth. "For whom am I toiling," he asked, "and why am I depriving myself of enjoyment?" This too is meaningless—a miserable business!*[2]

The situation is that there's a self-confessed workaholic. He's a guy who works really hard and has done well for himself. But now there's a problem: he can't remember why he's working. He asks for whom is he toiling, for what or rather, for whom is he working for? Is it for himself? Well it can't be, because he can't seem to enjoy any of the wealth that he has earned since he can't stop himself from working!

---

[2] Ecclesiastes 4:7-8, NIV.

It's like his work is making fun of him. He's got so much, yet he can't enjoy it. He's got himself trapped into this 'work-mode', stuck in a meaningless and miserable loop. Work, get money, feels like it is not enough, can't enjoy, work some more—and so the infinite cycle repeats itself.

Worse still, he's lonely. He is all alone, with neither son (either no time for marriage, or no time for kids) nor brother—probably because he has severed all his relationships and lost all his family ties because of his job. He's all alone.

He pursued work for so long in his life that he forgot what was important, and now he can't get it back. Now he's all alone and miserably lost. He can't seem to change anything, he couldn't even bring himself to re-prioritise or settle down even if he wanted to. Working forever, unable to enjoy anything; meaningless, all vanity—a chasing after the wind!

EVIL-WORK triggers the rat race. Life is placed in front of us, but it is illusory at best. The more we reach for it, the further it seems. The tighter we grip it, the faster it runs through our fingers. It is false hope, and yet, we can't seem to let it go! There is no other option.

Is there any way to exit the rat race once we start? Or are we trapped in it forever?

✋ | A Divine Interruption

Jesus will say this very bluntly:

Do not labor for the food that perishes...[1]

He warned us that if we spend all our energies doing this EVIL WORK, it will be laborious, difficult, stressful and anxiety-inducing. Yes, we may get some food, we may build some semblance of life, but in the end, there is only that miserable rat-race life in the present, perishing in the near future, and worse still, judgement in eternity.

Stop it, Jesus says.

Do not labour, Jesus says.

Jesus does not ask us to get better jobs or try some other career path. He is not criticising the type of job we have but rather, He is criticising the fact that all this striving is EVIL WORK. It is fuelled by sin and all the wrong motivations. It is the effort we are putting in to gain

---

[1] John 6:27

our own independent life—that is all EVIL WORK, no exceptions! We cannot produce our own lives; we never have and we never will. No matter how hard we work, we just end up dying faster. Rat-race work will kill you (and the others around you)—so stop it!

How, Jesus? We are stuck. How do we get out of this tyranny?

The crowds ask,

> *"What must we do, to be doing the works of God?"*
>
> *Jesus answered them, "This is the work of God, that you believe in him whom he has sent"*[2]

Take all that work, that labour, that toil, that sweat, that striving—and redirect it into trusting Me.

That's right. You know how much energy you put into your career to build up a life for yourself. Stop that completely; it's EVIL WORK. Now put that same time, energy and diligence into trusting Me.

This is the proper WORK of God.

Wow...that is pretty radical, wouldn't you say?

This is all happening when Jesus is feeding the five thousand, which should remind us of that original WORK-shop a thousand years earlier.

---

[2] John 6:28-29

Show me the Manna

Part 1: STOP

In Exodus, God saved His people through the blood of the firstborn lamb, and then desired them to Himself. Along the way, they had a very important lesson to learn, I dare say the most important lesson for living out the holy life: the lesson of the Manna.

Immediately after Egypt, they journeyed three months across a barren desert. It's hot—it's the Middle East after all—it's uncomfortable, you're walking around with three million people, huge numbers of smelly cows, goats and sheep...but the key thing is: there's no food.

> *Would that we had died by the hand of the L*ORD *in the land of Egypt, when we sat by the meat pots and ate bread to the full, for you have brought us out into this*

> *wilderness to kill this whole assembly with <u>hunger</u>.*[1]

The heat, crowds and especially hunger get to them and they begin to complain and complain—to the extent that they blame Moses and God[2] of wanting to kill them. Within a matter of days, they went from singing God's praises[3] to accusing Him of genocide.

Interestingly, the Lord accepts this blame. He did orchestrate this life-draining situation. He made them hunger on purpose:

> *And he humbled you and let you hunger and fed you with manna…that he might make you know that man does not live by bread alone, but man lives by every word that comes from the mouth of the LORD.*[4]

It's the same issue that Jesus mentioned in John 6: If you work to get food, to get your own life, you will die.

This is the EVIL-WORK.

The first lesson of the wilderness is to de-Egyptianise their thinking. Stop the rat-race logic in its tracks. Take away your ability to get your own food, create your own life. How do you work in the middle of the desert? You are left hungry and helpless. Death is seriously on the cards—hence their violent protests.

---

[1] Exodus 16:3
[2] Exodus 16:8
[3] Exodus 15
[4] Deuteronomy 8:3

There is a total loss of control and this is exactly where God wants you.

Wilderness moments are essential to destroy all that self-reliance—they bring you all the way down to nothingness; i.e., they humble you. That is the first lesson in the re-education of God's people...STOP!

God has got to take away everything—that's the only way you can leave the operating system of the world. He's got to be the one to take away all capacity to create life.

Wilderness today may look like job-loss, natural disaster, cancer, death in the family, injury, economic crisis, infertility, bankruptcy...the list goes on. Make no mistake, it is the Lord's doing, and the goal is the same: He's facilitating your exit from the rat race.

Now as we mentioned, the people can't take it. They grumble. Understandable. We all do. It is the natural frustration when your life is taken out of your own hands.

The lesson is not over, now comes...

Part 2: LOOK

God is not bothered with the grumbling. He now does something special: He rains the bread of angels[5] on their heads.

---

[5] Psalm 78:25

> *In the morning dew lay around the camp. And when the dew had gone up, there was on the face of the wilderness a fine, flake-like thing, fine as frost on the ground. When the people of Israel saw it, they said to one another, "What is it?" For they did not know what it was. And Moses said to them, "It is the bread that the LORD has given you to eat."*[6]

They go to sleep grumbling, but in the morning there's this frost-like thing on the ground. They all looked at this bizarre flour and asked, "What is it?"—which is the Hebrew word 'manna'—which became its official name. It was called the 'what is it' bread.

Imagine that conversation though....

> A: Hey what have you got there?
>
> B: What is it?
>
> A: Huh? I don't know. What is it?
>
> B: Yes, that's right.
>
> A: What is it?!!
>
> B: Yes!!

And so, the frustrations continue.

Anyway, they are given very specific instructions:

---

[6] Exodus 16:13–15

> *Gather of it, each one of you, as much as he can eat. You shall each take an omer, according to the number of the persons that each of you has in his tent...*[7]

Each was supposed to take an *omer* (about four litres of flour per person) of this divine-origin bread, more than enough for the day's needs. Just take for yourself (presumably for your children and dependents also) and eat all of it. Don't leave any extra for the next day.

Can you see what God is doing?

First, He stopped all your ability to do your EVIL-WORK, and when you are at the point of despair—He then sends a new source of life: bread from heaven—and it's just enough to get you to survive one day more.

Cancer enters remission, a new job offer comes through a headhunter's call, the economy picks up, foreign aid enters, the rains come after drought. The taking-away is replaced by giving of new unexpected gifts—things you never thought possible.

Life enters.

Unfortunately, the people don't understand. Some gathered more, some less[8]—this is probably an understatement. My guess is that what happens is chaos. Imagine one of those refugee settings. They have been starving and now the UN vehicles come in. What happens next?

---

[7] Exodus 16:16

[8] Exodus 16:17

Chaaaargeee.....

The stronger guys take way too much, the weaker probably get a lot less, people are pushing and shoving... what happens if there's not enough for me, my family? What about tomorrow? It's the rat race all over again!

Hard isn't it? To get that EVIL-WORK ethic out? But the stunning thing is, those who clearly took more than their fair share:

> ...had nothing left over, and whoever gathered little had no lack. Each of them gathered as much as he could eat.[9]

When they got home and measured it, it was exactly what each person was allocated: one *omer*. No more, no less.

Now isn't that exceptionally frustrating. I pushed and shoved to earn my 'more'. Yet I have exactly the same as the kid who took one wafer-cake.

Rat-race rules don't work in God's economy.

I suppose what happened next was that some ate less than an omer and attempted to store the rest for tomorrow—just in case right? After all, just because He gave us enough for today, there's no guarantee He'll give us enough tomorrow right?

> *Some left part of it till the morning, and it bred worms*

---

[9] Exodus 16:18–19

and stank. And Moses was angry with them.[10]

Nope...can't do that either. Can't store. Can't keep leftovers. It turns into hell.

Wait, wait...maybe there's another way. We just leave it on the ground, and when we want more we can get it later! Let's be sneaky about this.

Morning by morning, they gathered it...but when the sun grew hot, it melted.[11]

Oh boy...nothing's really working is it?

> Take more, get less.
> Store overnight, breeds worms.
> Leave for later, manna melts.

THIS...IS...IMPOSSIBLE!

I call it the ungraspable bread.

Are you getting the lesson yet?

Day 2, the same thing happens: You have to wait...bread of heaven falls from the sky.

Day 3, again: Wait, because God gives all you need and God takes away every bit of excess (whether you like it or not).

---

[10] Exodus 16:20
[11] Exodus 16:21

Day 4, again: Stop, look, receive.

Day 5 again, Day 6 again: God gives and God takes away.

Just think what this is teaching them. What are they learning?

Maybe Jesus gives us a clue here:

> *Do not be anxious about your life.... Look at the birds of the air: they neither sow nor reap <u>nor gather into barns</u>, and yet your heavenly Father feeds them. Are you not of more value than they?*
>
> *Why are you anxious about clothing? Consider the lilies of the field, how they grow: they <u>neither toil</u> nor spin...*[12]

Where does your life come from? Your work? Your efforts? Your storage? Really? The birds don't store, the flowers don't toil, but they are well taken care of, right?

Whether the people shook their fist or panicked in anxious fear, it didn't matter—God would still send the bread. Just relax...there will be enough bread, every day. Daily bread has been promised, daily bread will be delivered.

> *Do not labour for the food that perishes...*
> *Man does not live by bread alone...*
> *Do not be anxious about your life...*

---

[12] Matthew 6:25–33

Same lesson, no?

This is the key lesson that the people of God must learn, even before the ten commandments are given. Did you notice that? God doesn't start by giving people commandments to follow. He starts by teaching them how to trust Him. What's the use of giving people instructions—if they don't trust Him?

Trust Him first, then the commandments will make sense. Don't try to live the Christian life, until you trust the Christian God.

Trust me, lean back on me. I will give you all you need. Even when it seems like everything is out of control, I AM is still in control. And when everything *is* in control (when you think things are going well), don't be so silly to think that you are the one in charge of the orchestra. It's always been Me.[13]

Once we were cast out from Eden, we began to believe more and more that if I just work hard enough, I will have a good enough life. But this correlation is simply not true.

It's the same lesson that God continues to carry out in the land of Israel (another kind of Eden) later on. Whenever the people disobey or turn away from Him and pursue their own agendas much like Adam and Eve, one of the key things the Lord does is take away the rain.

I guess if we lived in an agricultural society we would see

---

[13] See Deuteronomy 8:11–20.

this clearer. I can plough the ground, plant the seeds, take care of the soil...but what if God doesn't send the rain? Then what? It doesn't matter how much I work, there will be no crops whatsoever![14]

When we stop serving God and keeping His ways, the heavens lock-up, the taps are switched off.[15] WORK (of any kind) can no longer be done. Drought and famine follow. This is a sure sign that Israel has headed towards the EVIL-WORK ethic, and now is the time to STOP and wait upon Him.

Think back to our parent-child reality. A child does not need to work to survive. A child survives purely on the labour of his/her parents. Everything is provided for daily, based on his/her parents' character and consistency. Life comes from the parents—regardless of what work this child does. Even if the child did absolutely nothing (which is basically what children do for the first 20 years of their lives) life *still* comes from the parents.

The great reformer Martin Luther once said, "God will not give [man] anything because of his labour, but solely out of His goodness and blessing".[16]

Throughout the six-day week the Lord has been giving and taking away, teaching His people that they don't need to WORK for their own life. Life comes from Him.

---

[14] Think back to the Genesis 2:5 initial description of work.

[15] For example, Deuteronomy 11:16-17; 28:23-24.

[16] Paul Althaus, *The Theology of Martin Luther* (Minneapolis, MN: Fortress Press, 1966), 109.

God has got to stop us in our tracks so that we can begin to re-direct our EVIL-WORK energies into trusting that He is true food and true drink. Or as Jesus put it:

> ...seek first his kingdom and his righteousness, and all these things will be <u>given</u> to you as well.[17]

The only Toil, Labour, Sweat kind of WORK in this age is the striving to trust God. The WORK is the fight against sin—the struggle to break our independent way of life.

A PERSONAL INTERRUPTION

Hard isn't it...to trust that everything in life comes from God?

It's not easy to learn this lesson, so that's why the Lord must teach us this lesson again and again and again. By giving and taking away through wilderness episodes.

In my life, I've had many such lessons. I remember during the year I got married, the Lord took away much of our finances. We went from very comfortable Singaporeans, to people who had to buy budget goods and soon-to-be expiring food. The Lord took away. Sure, we complained at first, but then we learned to trust Him a little bit more. In the end He surprised us with an incredible gift from unexpected sources when we were financially at our wits' end.

---

[17] Matthew 6:33, NIV.

The wilderness lessons didn't stop there. The most recent one was my health. For several months, I had been having a throat condition that limits the amount of speaking I can do each day. I mean for a pastor, your whole career is about speaking to people—whether that is one-to-one counselling, teaching Bible study classes, preaching, singing—your voice is your most important tool! So, when I started getting these pains, this long-term sore throat, I began to grumble: "Why is this happening to me? Can't the doctors figure it out? What do I pay you so much money for? Did you really go to medical school?!"

But who was I grumbling against? Was it the doctors? Did they give me the condition? Or was it God?

"Sure, you say you are a pastor, but will you trust Me if I even take your voice away? Will you trust that even without your voice I will still take care of you, I will still provide for your little children, I will still find you meaning and purpose—even if you cannot do your current job? Do you trust Me? Does your life come from your work or from Me?"

It is only when we finally begin to trust that He is the one who is in control and the only one who can give us life, that our EVIL-WORK ceases. The whole process of giving and taking away is to pry open our hands that have white-knuckle-gripped the reins of our own lives.

We start from an EVIL-WORK ethic, and God has to take away the rain for us to STOP.

- - - - - - - - - -

Part 3: GO

God is not done yet. It's not just about the giving and taking away. It's not just about the stopping and gathering. There's more He wants to show:

> *On the sixth day they gathered twice as much bread, two omers each. ..."Tomorrow is a day of solemn rest, a holy Sabbath to the LORD; bake what you will bake and boil what you will boil, and all that is left over lay aside to be kept till the morning." ..."Eat it today, for today is a Sabbath to the LORD; today you will not find it in the field. Six days you shall gather it, but on the seventh day, which is a Sabbath, there will be none."* [18]

After the six days, there will be a special day, a holy day, a REST day, called the Sabbath.

What do you do on the Sabbath?

> You stop labouring.
> You start enjoying.

At the end of the week, there will be a special day, where there is no need even to gather daily bread, but simply enjoy the *abundance* that the Lord provided (on the six days He catered to immediate needs). This time they could store two days' worth of food—and it wouldn't rot.

---

[18] Exodus 16:22–26

The Sabbath Day is a kind of divine celebration—it's God's gift to man.[19] No more WORK to be done, but a REST to be enjoyed. A time to savour all the WORK that had been done before.

It's very much like what God did on the first week of creation:

> *Six days you shall labor, and do all your work, but the seventh day is a Sabbath to the Lord your God. On it you shall not do any work, you, or your son, or your daughter, your male servant, or your female servant, or your livestock, or the sojourner who is within your gates. For in six days the Lord made heaven and earth, the sea, and all that is in them, and rested the seventh day. Therefore the Lord blessed the Sabbath day and made it holy.*[20]

God ceased from His creation work and rested, so you cease and rest. God enjoyed all his six days of labour—seeing it to be very good—so you enjoy all your six days of labour.

For six days man labours to trust God, that very sweaty work of striving and struggling against sin. But there is a promise that one day this will all cease. On the seventh day you could look forward to enjoy the full fruition of all that work.

There will be a time coming when there's nothing more to be done—and now we celebrate!

---

[19] Mark 2:27

[20] Exodus 20:9–11

A Vocational Interruption

When I just turned 30, I went for this course called Vocation, Work and Ministry.[21] It's a wonderful course, trying to understand not just the theology of work, but how we can make our own career or vocation decisions in life.

The course material aside, the thing that startled me was the participants. I was expecting the crowd to be full of 20 and 30-year-olds, those who are deciding on their degree course or entering their first or second job.

The surprising thing was that the majority of attendees were in their 50s and 60s. Was it that they had hit retirement or a dead end? No. They had all done stunningly well in their careers as doctors, lawyers, consultants, bankers; built mini-empires in their name; many were actively involved in church and had cultivated healthy nuclear families to boot. I would assume they had it sorted.

When the lecturer asked the class to detail why they had signed up for the course, it seemed that many still seemed unhappy, unfulfilled and even dreaded the inevitable time when they had to relinquish their positions because of age or illness. How could it be that people so seemingly successful were so obviously disillusioned?

I swore that would never happen to me. But how could I escape the same fate?

---

[21] Run by the Biblical School of Theology (BGST), Singapore.

There's a divine retirement coming, and one that's much better that our kind of retirement. Ever noticed that when people end work in this life (whether willingly or unwillingly)—it turns badly sour? It turns to resentment, bitterness, boredom, loneliness. Just think of the elderly epidemic the world now faces—that's EVIL-WORK retirement.

 # SABBATH^{x7}

The Sabbath is something completely different. A destination worth working for.

What *exactly* happens on the Sabbath?

There would be no labour, lots of food, lots of fellowship—with God and man.

It's basically a big party at the end of each week, where you invite your servants, the foreigner, the widow and the poor[1] to come and enjoy God's blessings with you—even the animals don't work!

As one author commented, there is "ceasing, resting, embracing and feasting."[2]

---

[1] Including the poor priests.
[2] For further reading, see Marva J. Dawn, *Keeping the Sabbath Wholly: Ceasing, Resting, Embracing, Feasting* (Grand Rapids, MI: Eerdmans, 1989).

Not only was this built into the weekly calendar, but the Sabbath then becomes the foundation for every one of Israel's celebration festivals, as we see in Leviticus 23.

Each occasion is done surrounding a Sabbath day, with each sharing some aspect of the coming REST time: Deliverance, Abundance, Forgiveness, Fellowship, Fruitfulness, Renewal, etc.[3]

It gets pretty crazy when you get to the Sabbath years. They would work six years in a row, but on the seventh year you do no work at all and enjoy free food for the entire 365 days[4] (the ground would produce enough crops for three years)![5]

And on the 49th year, you would again do the same for the 50th year.[6] That is to say both the 49th and 50th year would be Sabbath years (the 50th year is called the Jubilee Year). I don't know, maybe there's no productive work for four-to-five years in total?

Plus, on this Jubilee year, all kinds of Sabbath-y things would happen: slaves would be set free, debts would be cancelled, people would go home to their original properties and the whole country would be set right and enjoy great abundance.

---

[3] For further reading see Paul Blackham, *Book by Book: Leviticus*, (Sedona, AZ: Veritas, 2008).

[4] Leviticus 25:3–6

[5] Leviticus 25:21

[6] Leviticus 25:8–12

It was like a huge reset button was pressed, and the land magically transformed back into Eden-Paradise! God will just keep the food and drink flowing and flowing.

All this alluding to the fact that one day there would be a day of great enjoyment for God's people, a day that incorporated feasting, fellowship, freedom, righteousness, reward, reconciliation, and ultimately the removal of all EVIL. All that comes under the heading of 'Sabbath'.

A Crucial Interruption

In John 5, Jesus told us that:

My Father is always at his work to this very day, and I too am working.[1]

God ceased from His creation work all the way back in Genesis 2, but here we see that He's been constantly working every day since then or more specifically, every day since the Fall in Genesis 3.

God only stops work when everything is complete, when it is very good. So with the coming in of sin into the world of man, work begins again to eradicate all the evil. He labours diligently to shine His light into the darkness, to overcome evil with good, and His greatest most definitive work is sending His Son into the rat-pile to die on the cross.

---

[1] John 5.17, NIV.

God's WORK (toilsome labour) has always got to do with dealing with sin. It is the activity He does to give us life out of death.

That is why when preparing for the cross at Gethsemane, there was striving, anxiety, sweat,[2] thorns[3]—all the effects of EVIL-WORK—as the Lord prepares to kill that way of life.

After Jesus did His work at the cross, He sat down in heaven...it is finished.[4]

Adam, if we remember, was barred from the return to Eden with that flaming sword. Sin is not permitted to enter paradise. Yet with Jesus' work, the doorway to a renewed Edenic city is open. We may now enter God's REST once again, thanks to His WORK.

---

[2] Luke 22:44

[3] John 19:5

[4] Hebrews 10:12

Unrest, Redux

However, the Exodus Israelites didn't quite get this rest... they still wanted to work:

> *On the seventh day some of the people went out to gather, but they found none. And the LORD said to Moses, "How long will you refuse to keep my commandments and my laws? See! The LORD has given you the Sabbath; therefore on the sixth day he gives you bread for two days. Remain each of you in his place; let no one go out of his place on the seventh day." So the people rested on the seventh day.*[1]

Moses was absolutely furious that they would reject such a tremendous gift from God! So much so that he made breaking the Sabbath a death-penalty law,[2] and later we see it in action:

---

[1] Exodus 16:27–30
[2] Exodus 31:15–17

> *While the people of Israel were in the wilderness, they found a man gathering sticks on the Sabbath day. And those who found him gathering sticks brought him to Moses and Aaron and to all the congregation. They put him in custody, because it had not been made clear what should be done to him. And the LORD said to Moses, "The man shall be put to death; all the congregation shall stone him with stones outside the camp."*[3]

Why so serious?

Because if the Sabbath was God's gift of REST to man, then to work on the Sabbath would be a rejection of all the work that God did to gain us this future. Just like in Eden, God worked to provide a paradise-home for His little children, and they rejected it—starting an EVIL-WORK of wanting to be their own gods.

So also, to work on the Sabbath would imply exactly the same thing: I want out and I want it my way. The prodigal son rejects Sabbath life and runs.

To reject Sabbath is to reject God's salvation, God's deliverance, even God's cross! That's why when the ten commandments were rewritten in Deuteronomy 5, did you notice the change of rationale for the Sabbath law?

> *Six days you shall labor and do all your work, but the seventh day is a Sabbath to the LORD your God. On it you shall not do any work, you or your son or your*

---

[3] Numbers 15:32–35

daughter or your male servant or your female servant, or your ox or your donkey or any of your livestock, or the sojourner who is within your gates, that your male servant and your female servant may rest as well as you. You shall remember that you were a slave in the land of Egypt, and the L<small>ORD</small> your God brought you out from there with a mighty hand and an outstretched arm. Therefore the L<small>ORD</small> your God commanded you to keep the Sabbath day.[4]

God did a mighty work to deliver you—so you must keep the Sabbath!

Furthermore, in the prophets, we see that Sabbath-keeping is deeply tied into practices of righteousness, justice and holy living, for example:

- In Isaiah 48, Sabbath-keeping is tied to loosing the bonds of wickedness and letting the oppressed go free.

- In Amos 8, those that can't wait for the Sabbath to end quickly proceed to profiteering and deceitful business practices.

- In Nehemiah 13, he threatens violence against Sabbath market-sellers because he knows that will send the nation back into its horrible slave trading past.[5]

- In Deuteronomy 15, those that fear the seventh year

---

[4] Deuteronomy 5:13-15
[5] See Nehemiah 5:5.

Sabbath 'refund policy', are seen as those who are calculative towards the poor.

Many times in Israel's history, we see that once the Sabbath is not kept—Israel descends into the rat race once more. It becomes a dog-eat-dog nation, even worse than the nations around them.

To reject Sabbath is to reject the work that God did to grant us rest. Those that didn't practise Sabbath were insistent on going the way of the world, and thus were to be permanently excommunicated from the family of God.

Which is why the book of Hebrews warns the New Testament church, that if you want to enter His REST— you must cease from all your EVIL-WORK:

> *...for whoever has entered God's rest has also rested from his works as God did from his. Let us therefore strive to enter that rest...*[6]

As Jesus said: labour to trust Him. The prime work of humanity in the sinful age is to strive to enter this rest. Ironically, we work to cease from our own work.

As mentioned, God's WORK has always got to do with dealing with sin.

---

[6] Hebrews 4:10–11

⌖ Re-Orientation

Not surprisingly then, to keep Sabbath properly is to acknowledge God's WORK, God's deliverance and God's salvation. In today's language, it is to keep the cross firmly fixed in view. God has done His work, He is still doing His work, and one day all His work will cease – and we can enjoy His Rest, with Him.

Sabbath is a day the church comes together and remembers what God has worked for us—all aspects of the cross (as coloured by the Leviticus festivals)—and does everything to look forward or to point towards that coming REST time.

The Heidelberg Catechism phrases it best:

> Q. What is God's will for you in the fourth commandment?
>
> A. First, that the gospel ministry and education for it be maintained, and that, especially on the festive day of rest, I diligently attend the assembly of God's people to learn what God's Word teaches,

> to participate in the sacraments, to pray to God publicly, and to bring Christian offerings for the poor.
>
> Second, that every day of my life I rest from my evil ways, let the Lord work in me through his Spirit, and so begin in this life the eternal Sabbath.[1]

I think that's a great summary of what should happen on the Sabbath: rest, festivities, hearing from God, enjoying sacraments, making sure that the poor can join in, ceasing from EVIL-WORK, looking forward to the ETERNAL Sabbath—the time when REST is the new norm, in the new creation. The time when all of God's work comes to full fruition.

The practise of Sabbath keeping becomes a re-orienting tool in the life of the church, something that keeps us remembering God's WORK of deliverance, and God's gift of REST that is certainly coming.

I guess that's why Sabbath was shifted from the end of the week to the beginning of the week in the New Testament calendars.[2] It was meant to be an empowering thing to fuel our current working lives.

Without Sabbath—we harden our rat-race instincts. Practising Sabbath is key to our exit strategy.

---

[1] Question 103.

[2] Many have stated that the Saturday Sabbath was then replaced by the Sunday Lord's Day. Although strictly speaking the New Testament allows us to be quite flexible on Sabbath practise—as long as we actually do something!

 **REST FUEL**

As God gives and takes away, we learn (assuming we are hearing His Word) to trust and lean back in the God who works for us. As we receive and practice the gift of Sabbath, we look forward to the kind of life He has been preparing for us since the foundation of the world.[1]

Yet ceasing from the EVIL-WORK, as toilsome and sweaty as that is, is not God's only goal. He has obviously prepared GOOD-WORK for us to do.

Let's go back to the story of the prodigal son. The son, in running away from home, comes under the curse; all his work is doomed to fail. He has to stop. He has to remember his father. He has to come home. He has to receive. He has to rest in his father's love.

But now imagine, what happens next? Surely the father would say that he has GOOD-WORK for him to do.

GOOD-WORK comes out of *enjoying* the Father's REST.

---

[1] Hebrews 4:3

GOOD-WORK will be in line with the Father's WORK—getting them to cease, *pointing others* to His REST.

GOOD-WORK is not about *earning* life (the son already has life); GOOD-WORK is about *sharing* life.

It's the kind of work Jesus did—the good works of God[2]—and they all have to do with giving others life ~~from death~~. And what's more, Jesus said His church will do the same, if not *greater works*[3] than He did!

That GOOD-WORK as we have seen is not really defined by simply having a moral career, but rather a work that is fuelled by the right motivation and does not come under the curse.

All EVIL-WORK is fuelled by the desire to be our own gods, to take charge of our own destiny, and these must cease. Once we cease, and rest in Him, trust that He is taking care of our own life. Now we are ready to do GOOD-WORK for the life of others—fuelled by His love, motivated by His compassion, empowered by His Spirit and aiming for His glory.

These are the only works that are recorded in eternity, tested by fire and not burned, regarded as 'something'.[4] Let me give you an example:

I'm a pastor—so naturally all my work should be

---

[2] For example, John 10:32.

[3] John 14:12

[4] John 15:5

GOOD-WORK right?

Wrong.

I have learned over the years that when I write great sermons (based on feedback from the congregation), there are two ways I have fuelled them.

The first fuel is often anxiety. I have a deadline, I need to write something, I stress myself out, I worry about how it's going to sound, and I use that unease to push a sermon out. Surprisingly, the greater the anxiety, the better the sermon (at least in a superficial way) because I am most worried about what others will think.

Yet after the sermon is done, although I feel temporarily relieved, I then enter a new round of stress: waiting for the feedback, avoiding eye contact, dreading the next email, reacting strongly to criticism, lacking the ability to hold affirmation… and the last thing I want to do is spend time praying and thanking God. I just want to curl up with Netflix and a heavy meal—it's over! It was an EVIL-WORK, and the results—no matter how good it sounded—were only evil.

The second way I could write that sermon, is being fuelled by God's love. I stop, put my work aside, get out my Bible and pray. I remind myself that I am God's sheep first, before being a shepherd. I remember all the good things He has already done, as well as all the times He has delivered my sermons for me and ministered to me through His words. I consider His heart for me and I extrapolate that to the rest of the congregation.

After that, I proceed to think about the text and what He's saying to me first, rather than how to 'sermon-ise' it. Now a new flavour appears: I think about the pastoral condition of my flock, I remember people whom certain words may hurt or trigger, others that need comfort or reassurance. The sermon is no longer delivered to stem my anxiety, but to minister to the lost and struggling.

Not as flashy as the first, but infinitely more powerful. I am less reactive to both good or bad feedback. I can look people in the eye and want to have follow-up conversations. People find that they are less impressed but more cut or consoled. I find myself going back to God in prayer and sincere thanksgiving—not so much about the sermon delivery but the fact that I knew He was with me in the process. I go back to resting again in His tender care and words: GOOD-WORK, my faithful servant...

The first sermon came out of UNREST and led to EVIL. The second sermon came out of God's REST and hopefully pointed others to that same REST.

Just because someone brings order, or volunteers, or creates efficiency; is a campaigner for social justice, makes beautiful music or art, brings deep insight; builds a team, outlines a vision, acts as a peacemaker—it doesn't make it GOOD-WORK, and it certainly doesn't make it GOD-WORK. What's the fuel behind it? That is the key question.

Recently I've been doing a lot of 'deep work' with individuals, getting behind anger outbursts, depression, panic attacks, sexual deviancy, addictions and so forth. Many of them are extremely successful in their careers and outer life. But when we begin to explore what's underneath—the causes behind their issues—it all boils down to the same root. What drove those empire-building efforts was not Jesus' work on the cross—it was not a work stemming from the REST of God, and so it warped their (or our) whole being. More than ever, I can see why Jesus will not accept *any* of these works on Judgement Day; they are completely toxic and have nothing to do with the Kingdom.

Martin Luther once stated that any work that is taking us away from God is an evil work and a mortal (deadly) sin.[5]

GOOD-WORK is not about earning life we don't have. GOOD-WORK is about sharing life we already have.

Which is why it's no surprise that Jesus can do all kinds of work on the Sabbath Day, and yet never be breaking the Sabbath! When He was not in a good place, He took time to keep the Sabbath (see His extended retreats in

---

[5] For further reading, see Martin Luther, *Heidelberg Disputation*, 1519.

Luke's gospel), until He could once again minister. Every work that Jesus did was from a place of God's rest, and that's why every work that Jesus did was not placed under the Genesis 3 curse, even the cross. All His works were blessed and everything He did prospered!

Jesus was often called the blessed man; everything He did turned out well.[6] When the blessed man came and didn't like the weather, He could rebuke the wind and the waves and they would do as they were told. When He was on the other side of the lake, He could either tell the water to turn solid to walk over or He could just teleport the boat. When He wanted food, all He had to do was pray—He had a single packed lunch and kept sharing it out—and He had enough to feed thousands. No toil, no sweat. The earth just kept giving it to Him, as much food or water as He wanted. Even the finest wine, no problem. Six hundred litres? Easy!

Everything worked for Him—there was no painful toil, there was no decay, there was no loss or brokenness. Wherever He needed to be, whatever He needed to happen, whatever He wanted to do, it just prospers. He just does all things well. Isn't that incredible? That's life under the continuous blessing of God.

If we want any of our works, careers, unpaid work, ministries, volunteerism, or service to be blessed and established (to not come under the curse of futility) then it has to be a GOOD-WORK, not an EVIL-WORK. It has to be a work undergirded by God's ministry to us first.

---

[6] Mark 7:37

Or to use agricultural language: He sends the rain, we work the ground.[7]

Martin Luther once said, "Govern, and let Him give blessing. Fight and let Him give victory. Preach, and let Him win hearts. And so on. In all our doings He is to work through us, and He alone shall have the glory from it".[8]

In fact, that was what Israel learned in the land of Canaan; it only rained when they served God and kept His commandments.[9] When they trusted God, rested in Him, then and only then, did fruitfulness happen in every sphere of life—and it was almost effortless.[10]

Or as Jesus put it, God's work is easy work;[11] it is not meant to be burdensome.[12] The only toilsome work in the gospel is the sweaty work of fighting against sin as Jesus demonstrated at Gethsemane. Everything else is light.

When we do GOOD WORK, it is always about sharing what we already have. Imagine back in the Exodus desert: if the people finally learned that God would take care of all their needs, how do you think their gathering of the manna would change?

---

[7] Genesis 2:5

[8] Paul Althaus, *The Theology of Martin Luther* (Minneapolis, MN: Fortress Press, 1966), 109.

[9] See Deuteronomy 11.

[10] See Deuteronomy 28.

[11] Matthew 11:29–30

[12] 1 John 5:3

It wouldn't be rat-race push and shove. It would be taking as much as they needed, and if they happened to get excess, they would share it gladly with the other who still needed. No one would dream of storing up—what would be the point?

That's exactly how the apostle Paul applies it:

> *Your abundance at the present time should supply their need, so that their abundance may supply your need, that there may be fairness. As it is written, "Whoever gathered much had nothing left over, and whoever gathered little had no lack."*[13]

The more we work this way, the more there will be no poor amongst God's people—everyone will have their needs taken care of.[14]

But if we don't trust Him, no matter how hard we work, no matter how noble our career, it never seems to be enough; money disappears as though in a bag with holes,[15] the locusts eat all our fruit, nothing satisfies, and we get more and more selfish. Might as well not work if God is not in the picture; there's no use in the long run.

Learn to rest first, then work later!

The true race, is the REST-RACE.

---

[13] 2 Corinthians 8:14–15

[14] See Deuteronomy 15, and also how Exodus 16 is quoted as the basis for 2 Corinthians 8.

[15] See Haggai 1.

 **SELAH**

We learn how to Sabbath by keeping a fixed day with lots of fixed rituals (I strongly recommend this to start). We start by rote learning and forced movements like Sunday church services, fixed quiet times, regular retreats, as well as scheduled Christian small groups.[1]

Hopefully we can then graduate into a more natural rhythm. A rhythm that can be practiced any day, any time. A rhythm that should get stronger and sharper and which shapes more of our lifestyles the more mature we get.

The great theologian Dietrich Bonhoeffer said:

> Has [the time alone with God] transported him for a moment into a spiritual ecstasy that vanishes

---

[1] For further reading see: Soo-Inn Tan, *3-2-1: Following Jesus in Threes* (Singapore: Graceworks, 2013).

when everyday life returns, or has it lodged the Word of God so securely and deeply in his heart that it holds and fortifies him, impelling him to active love, to obedience, to good works? Only the day [and time alone with God] can decide. I need to receive before I can give I need to be loved before I can love I need to be held before I can open my arms.[2]

It's not so easy to build a personal rhythm of Stop, Look, Go. It takes a lot of practice. We need to have a high degree of self-awareness (which ironically comes when others point things out).

So whenever I sense myself doing an EVIL-WORK (when I feel anxiety, competition, stress; guilt, shame, jealousy or fear taking over), I stop. I cease. I take the time to receive good things from God—in prayer, in song, in worship; in Scripture, in conversation with a Christian brother or sister, or in enjoying His creation.

I remember what God has worked for me, I remember who He is, I delight in the fact of the eternal Sabbath which is a gift prepared for me. I take this joy as my strength. Then I go, I move, I act. I resolve to help my brother or sister, to love my neighbour.

Some call this movement a 'Selah' movement (as in the Psalms).

---

[2] Dietrich Bonhoeffer, *Life Together* (San Francisco, CA: HarperOne, 2009), 88.

 I Stop

 I Receive (Look)

 I Go

Have you found your Selah movement yet?

> *This is the work of God, that you believe in him whom he has sent.*[3]

It takes practice, it takes time, and it takes work. Remember we are steeped in the EVIL-WORK rat-race ethic from birth, so you will soon realise the amount of striving needed—to redirect all those EVIL-WORKs into Christ, so that a new GOOD-WORK can be born—is tremendous.

Thankfully, Jesus is very patient with us, and very gentle:

> *Come to me, all who labour and are heavy laden, and I will give you rest. Take my yoke upon you, and learn from me, for I am gentle and lowly in heart, and you will find rest for your souls. For my yoke is easy, and my burden is light.*[4]

---

[3] John 6:29
[4] Matthew 11:28–30

Back to the Question

Are we made to WORK or to REST?

Do you Work to Rest or Rest to Work?

Well...I think I've written enough. So why not take some time to think about this yourself or with some good friends?

1. What is the difference between a good work and an evil work?
2. How can I diagnose when I am doing a good work or an evil work?
3. How does my career fit into this? What if it doesn't fit?
4. What is my current understanding of Sabbath?
5. What are my current rest practices?
6. How can I have better rhythms of 'Stop, Look, Go'?
7. Who can keep encouraging me to think this way?

GRACEW♥RKS

Graceworks is a publishing and training consultancy based in Singapore, dedicated to promoting spiritual friendship in church and society, and seeing lives transformed through books that present truth for life.

Our publications can be found on our online store, *www.graceworks.com.sg/store*. Paperbacks are also available on Bookdepository and Amazon and eBooks on Kindle, iBooks, Google Play and Kobo.

You can contact us at *enquiries@graceworks.com.sg*, or follow us on Facebook (@GraceworksSG) and Instagram (graceworkssg).

www.ingramcontent.com/pod-product-compliance
Lightning Source LLC
LaVergne TN
LVHW041225080526
838199LV00083B/3321